# Understanding
# *BALLET*

This edition published 1972 by
OCTOPUS BOOKS LIMITED,
30 Bouverie Street, London, E.C.4.

Originally published 1965 by
Oldbourne Book Co. Ltd.

ISBN 7064 0021 6

Printed in Hong Kong.

# Understanding BALLET

## The steps of the dance from classroom to stage

Text by
### JOHN GREGORY

Photographs by
### MIKE DAVIS

OCTOPUS BOOKS LIMITED
London · New York · Sydney · Hong Kong

# CONTENTS

Eva Evdokimova, recipient of the Varna Gold Medal (1970), and ballerina of the Deutsche Oper. Her unique qualities have been likened to those of Taglioni

*Giselle,* Act II. Belinda Wright and Anton Dolin

# How to enjoy ballet

Today, so much is written, or criticized about ballet that it has become almost like a surgical operation, a vivisection of the anatomy of the human being.

Why not for once try and enjoy the beautiful art of the dance without everlastingly dissecting its limitations or adding with similar words its attributes? Why not for once, let us say we enjoy ballet, because of the beauty, the feminine charm and the athletic strength it can bring to the average uninitiated onlooker?

Ballet can give us the sound of music allied to the beauty of movement as no other art is able to.

What can be more beautiful than the joy derived from the classic ballet unimpaired by the everlasting message of the kitchen sink?

Ballet is, or should be, the most health-giving exercise both for the artist who dances and the audience who witnesses the performance. Simplicity in form seems to have been forgotten. Subjects that are so foreign to the art of the dance are prevalent and fail miserably at the box office.

Beauty and magic that true ballet can conjure up are too often set aside to enable the personal whim of the choreographer to have its sway.

I deplore the changing of the great classics, whether by the young who know no better or by the older who certainly should. Who would dare change a note of a Beethoven or Tchaikovsky symphony or change the colour or figures of a Goya or Raphael masterpiece? Of course we must find new ballets, new subjects, but let them be balletic, using the basic technique of the dance, a heritage that has been handed to the English dancer and dance and one to be faithfully guarded, not thrown aside.

For these reasons I have faith in 'Harlequin' and his magic wand.

ANTON DOLIN

Dame Alicia Markova, the English girl who danced with the Russian Ballet, and later achieved a name as legendary as Pavlova. After her retirement from dancing she became Ballet Director at the 'Met' and is now Professor of Ballet at Cincinatti University

# Introduction

How often after a performance of ballet we hear the remark, 'I like ballet, but I don't understand it', or 'I enjoyed it although I don't know what it is all about'.

Such comments suggest a desire to know more about an art whose mystery has a very wide appeal.

Ballet has in its make-up elements of all the arts: dancing, drama, poetry, literature, painting, sculpture, design and, of course, music. Because of its rhythmical nature its benefits are manifold and the training of eye and ear is of immense value in developing aesthetic appreciation.

For the average person to enjoy a ballet it is not essential to have a knowledge of the technique and mechanics of the art. The human instinct can respond quite easily to the sensibilities of sight and sound. Nevertheless, one of the joys of living is finding out how things work–almost everybody has a desire to see behind the scenes–and to understand what makes things 'tick'.

To be able to appraise a ballet, to be able to savour more fully the qualities of a work, to be able to distinguish good dancing from bad, one must acquire a knowledge of its medium, and a grasp of the conventions and symbols within that medium.

In this volume we are endeavouring to explain in simple language with graphic illustrations the principles of the classical dance from the basic exercises of the classroom to the interpretation of classical ballet on the stage in its many forms and variations.

*Les Sylphides*, Fokine's classical ballet of the romantic period

# History

Before considering the structure of ballet it is advantageous to know something of its history and development. Although ballet as we know it today is a young art, its roots go back to ancient terpsichore, emanating from the traditions of Egyptian and Greek cultures.

In the sixteenth and seventeenth centuries it sprang up in Italy under the patronage of a noble family, the Medicis. It spread to France, and later became a cult of the French Court. Louis xiv, known as the Sun King, opened the first Academy of Dance in 1661 and imported Italian ballet masters. Under such ballet masters as Beauchamp, Pecour and Feuillet it began to be developed into a serious art.

It was not long before European ballet masters travelled from one court to another. The Empress Anne introduced ballet to Russia, and engaged French ballet masters.

During the eighteenth century ballet waxed strong in France with such great masters as Jean-Georges Noverre, the Vestris, Gardel, Dauberville, Didelot. The influence of the elegant French school spread far and wide. By the nineteenth century, ballet was developing in many European capitals, most conspicuously in Rome, Florence, Vienna, Paris, London, and Copenhagen.

In Copenhagen ballet reached new heights under a great master by name of August Bournonville. Bournonville's pupil Christian Johansson took the gracious Bournonville style to Russia at the end of the last century.

During the same period in Italy the technique of ballet had made tremendous advances under the influence of Carlo Blasis, and from Italy Enrico Cecchetti was to take the brilliant technical and acrobatic school to Moscow and St Petersburg.

The Russian masters developed from the two great schools a master system of training which for the past eighty years has created the greatest dancers the world has ever known.

It happened then that while the French ballet was falling into a state of decline the Russians were busy bringing ballet to a high state of perfection.

As well as the Imperial Ballet of the court, many wealthy landowners had their own serf ballets. The Russians produced a race of dancers and earned themselves the title of 'born dancers'.

In 1909 the impresario, Serge Diaghilev, brought some members of the Imperial Ballet to Paris. The impact was breathtaking – such superb dancing had never been seen before in the Western world, and a great era of Russian ballet sprang up powered by *emigré* Russians. From these troupes such names as Pavlova, Nijinsky, Kschesinska, and Karsavina have become legendary.

In the 1930s regular seasons of Russian Ballet were given in London and

New York by Col. de Basil's Ballet Russe, and from this era the names of Massine, Balanchine, Dolin, Danilova, Markova, Riabouchinska, and Toumanova became famous.

During the '30s British ballet was also beginning to take root at the Sadler's Wells Theatre in London, and also at the Mercury Theatre where Dame Marie Rambert was nurturing the Ballet Rambert.

Dame Ninette de Valois, a ballerina who had danced with the Diaghilev Company, organized a small troupe of dancers, at first known as the Vic-Wells Ballet, which was to grow into the large and famous company we know today as the Royal Ballet.

Dame Ninette wisely built the foundation of her repertoire on the Russian classics and added ballets of a native flavour, such as her own *The Rake's Progress*, *Checkmate*, and *Job*, and she gave Sir Frederick Ashton the opportunity to make numerous ballets. He developed into a prolific choreographer of outstanding abilities, and his full-length classics, *Cinderella*, *Ondine*, and *La Fille Mal Gardée* have earned for him world-wide fame.

Many of Ashton's ballets were designed for the Company's prima ballerina Dame Margot Fonteyn, one of the most exquisite dancers of this century.

Anton Dolin formed the Festival Ballet which enjoyed many years of international success. It continues today under the direction of Beryl Grey, a former ballerina of the Royal Ballet.

Just as England has been largely influenced by the Russian heritage, America also has been dependent upon the Russians for the introduction of some of the finest ballets, and Russian *emigré* teachers have helped greatly in building up a native school of dancers. Mikhail Mordkin was the first Russian to make an American Ballet Company in the '30s, and one of his dancers was Lucia Chase who later was to found and direct American Ballet Theatre. Lincoln Kirstein, a connoisseur of the arts, was largely responsible for the formation of New York City Ballet, and for persuading George Balanchine to become its director and principal choreographer.

Since then ballet in America has prospered and proliferated until almost every town and city of importance has its own civic or regional ballet. Probably the generous grants given by the Ford Foundation have stimulated the upsurge during the past ten years. Ballet has become so fashionable in New York that it is able to support two major companies running simultaneously along with numerous Modern dance groups, for long seasons in winter, summer, and autumn.

America's two leading companies, Ballet Theatre and New York City Ballet, are comparable with the world's greatest. Both have a complement of brilliant virtuoso dancers, augmented with international guest stars, and both have vast repertoires of classics and contemporary works of lasting merit.

# The Dancers

Dancers are the living material of a ballet; they are the physical means, the malleable substance which the choreographer moulds into a composition of expressive movement.

The dancer has to be an artist, an athlete, and an acrobat, and to enable him or her to perform the difficult feats they are called upon to execute, they have to practise several hours every day of their lives.

The training of a dancer takes ten years, but in fact it is never finished. Most of our young dancers embark upon a stage career after three or five years of full-time training. The going is hard, usually a gruelling life in a corps de ballet for some years, but with determination and luck comes eventual promotion to the rank of soloist, and eventually, but only for the most talented, the coveted title of ballerina.

A great deal of the female dancer's life is spent practising to dance gracefully on the point of the toe. The male, who never dances on the toe and never should, spends almost as much time learning to hold, lift and turn a ballerina as he does to develop his own virile dancing technique.

Today, happily, the male dancer is coming into his own. It is true that not enough men of the right physical calibre take up ballet in England, and we are largely dependent upon the Commonwealth to supply us with sufficient male strength. All the same, a great advance in masculinity and technical prowess is evident.

The name Rudolf Nureyev has become famous in English ballet. A Russian dancer of splendid gifts, he is a somewhat undisciplined genius who has injected new life into our ballet scene. The Russian dancers are endowed with a musicality and grace that makes their dancing utterly harmonious and satisfying and performances by visiting companies have been a great inspiration.

American dancers are noted for their technical accomplishment, their virility and athletic prowess. As yet the lyric qualities of the Romantic ballet seem to evade them; on the other hand they have a positive flair for parody. Possibly the influence of the recently acquired Natalia Makarova formerly of the Kirov, with her superb artistry and style will have as great an effect upon American ballerinas as Nureyev did upon the English male dancer.

Important as the school is in raising and developing dancers, it is the talent that is most vital; and great talent is most rare. But despite this fact, it has been proved that the exceptional artist dancer will find her way through. The genius will break out regardless of good or bad schooling. The point is that a Pavlova, a Nijinsky, a Kschesinska, a Karsavina or a Fonteyn is a rare phenomenon.

Lucette Aldous and Ben Stevenson: *Pas de deux* from *Sleeping Beauty* (Festival Ballet)

Margot Fonteyn and Rudolf Nureyev in *Corsair*, one of the most popular dances of this famous partnership (following pages)

Suzanne Farrell formerly Balanchine's favourite ballerina, at present dancing with Maurice Béjart's Ballet of the XX Century

Irina Kolpakova, one of the Kirov Ballet's brightest jewels, as Princess Aurora

Natalia Makarova famous ballerina of the Kirov Ballet, Leningrad, now with the American Ballet Theatre. The picture shows her in one of her greatest roles *The Black Swan*

Margot Fonteyn and Rudolf Nureyev, the magic partnership

Left: Violette Verdy and Edward Villella two of New York City Ballet's brightest stars, in a *Grand Pas de Deux* given at a Royal Gala in London's Coliseum

Two dramatic studies: Fonteyn and Nureyev in *Marguerite and Armand*. This ballet was specially created for them by Sir Frederick Ashton (following pages)

Another interpretation of Shakespeare's play *Romeo and Juliet*. Tchaikovsky's music. Belinda Wright and Jelko Yuresha, Yugoslav dancer

Fonteyn and Nureyev in another immortal love-story, *Romeo and Juliet*: choreography, Kenneth McMillan. Royal Ballet production

George Balanchine one of the most prolific choreographers of all time, caught during a break in rehearsals. Among his well known works in the international repertoire are: *Serenade*, *Concerto Barocco*, *Apollo*, *Theme and Variations*, *Prodigal Son*, *Four Temperaments*, *Symphony in C*, *Divertimento*, and many, many more

Jerome Robbins, America's own genius of the dance. He grew up with Ballet Theatre for whom he choreographed such exciting ballets as *Interplay* and *Fancy Free*. Later he choreographed Musicals including *West Side Story* and *Fiddler on the Roof*. Had his own Company, Ballets U.S.A. Recently he has choreographed several ballets for New York City Ballet, two of the most remarkable being *Dances at a Gathering* and the *Goldberg Variations*

# Choreography

The creator of a ballet is the choreographer. He uses movement patterns to develop a theme, or tell a story. Some ballets interpret a mood, while others are merely an evocation of beauty, an expression of an idea or novelty; but whatever the ballet, it requires a vocabulary of movement to set it in motion. Movement is everything! The connoisseur of ballet must develop a discriminating eye for movement.

As I have intimated, the actual language of dance may be used in many meanings, in many combinations, in many derivations and styles. It is unnecessary to look for too exact a meaning. Like any word used verbally, the choreographies (steps or movements) are used by different artists in different ways. Any work of art conveys particular emotions and meanings to individual beings. This is the universality of art.

It will be seen how the classroom steps and exercises become fragments of choreography. By more elaborate combinations and by the weaving of intricate patterns, the work of the classroom or workshop is projected on to the stage; by means of a collaboration of choreographer, musicians, dancers, designers, and technicians a ballet takes shape.

The development of choreography has followed closely the development of music. The dances of the fourteenth, fifteenth, and sixteenth centuries were social dances and the music was composed for these dances—the early Basse dance is a simple walking dance, rather grave, the Bransles are more gay, the Galliard is again a serious dance, the Jig or the Rigaudon a jolly dance.

With each century the music and dance developed together with more invention and decoration. The Minuet became a popular dance of many intricate and charming variations. Then came the more sophisticated Gavotte, and other dances of the court.

At the same time the Folk dances (the dances of the people) also developed and spread, cultivating with Folk music and costumes a colourful and virile art form. Both these streams have contributed greatly to the enrichment of ballet and music.

By the nineteenth century ballet was becoming the art of the Opera House, and composers were commissioned to write special scores for ballet. Many full-length ballets appeared. Adam's *Giselle*, Delibes' *Coppelia*, Pugni's *Esmeralda*, Drigo's *Millions of Harlequin*, Glazunov's *Raymonda*, to mention but a few. Then came the greatest ballet composer of all—

Tchaikovsky, with *Swan Lake* (the most famous of all ballets), *The Nut-cracker*, and *The Sleeping Beauty*.

The turn of the century was the greatest period of the Romantic ballet. Marius Petipa and Lev Ivanov were two of Russia's greatest choreographers of the nineteenth century, the originators of *Swan Lake* and *The Sleeping Beauty*. Following them came Michel Fokine whose work was to achieve world fame, the creator of *Les Sylphides* and a host of ballets all of different genres: *Spectre de la Rose* (Weber), *Firebird* (Stravinsky), *Le Coq d'Or* ('Golden Cockerel') (Rimsky-Korsakov), *Petrushka* and many, many other ballets most of which are lost to us today.

In our century Stravinsky, Rachmaninoff, Prokofiev, Britten are some of the musical giants, and Ashton, Massine, Lifar, Balanchine, Lavrowsky, Lander are some of the greatest choreographers who have created lasting works in the classical medium.

The choreography of the nineteenth century was formal and symmetrical, the dance of the twentieth century has struck out at many different tangents enlarging the vocabulary—developing larger and more spectacular patterns, aerial lifts, and acrobatic combinations. Where movement is square or angular it shows the neo-classic trend. Like architecture, today's choreography is inclined to scramble and meander in a profusion of eccentricities.

In looking at a performance of a ballet, the spectator should endeavour to adjust his ears to the music and assimilate the relationship of the sound with the movement and the drama, remembering that in a well-made ballet the music dictates the shape and pattern of the dance, remembering also that without music dance would be limited, lacking in inspiration and in danger of monotony.

Festival Ballet's production of *Swan Lake*, Act II

Two beautiful studies of Eva Evdokimova and Cyril Atanasoff in *Giselle*. Their performances in London as guest stars with Festival Ballet received rave notices from the critics

Dame Alicia Markova, most famous Sylphide of all time, with John Gilpin in *Les Sylphides*

Antoinette Sibley and Anthony Dowell of the Royal Ballet in *Swan Lake*

Jane Langdon, top student of Royal Ballet, now soloist in the Company, as Aurora; the first time a student has ever danced the leading role at the School performance

Two pictures of *Trinity*, a ballet of youth by Gerald Arpino, chief choreographer and assistant director of the Robert Joffrey City Center Ballet of New York, an all American company that has come to the fore and won international acclaim in the U.S.S.R. and Europe. Centre in the lower picture is Christian Holder, principal dancer of the company

Scene from the Festival Ballet's production of *The Nutcracker*, another Tchaikovsky ballet particularly beloved by children

Galina Samtsova, Kiev-trained Russian ballerina from Canada now ballerina of Festival Ballet, in *Giselle*, Act I

*Bourrée Fantasque*, by the great classical choreographer George Balanchine, who has for many years directed the New York City Ballet

*La Fille Mal Gardée*, Ashton's greatest full-length ballet, with Nadia Nerina and David Blair: a magnificent ballet full of colour, humanity and gaiety (right)

Two young British dancers who are real favourites with American audiences, Antoinette Sibley and Anthony Dowell in Kenneth MacMillan's production of *Romeo and Juliet*

Suzanne Farrell in Balanchine's classic *Apollo*

Danish Erik Bruhn, guest star of American Ballet Theatre, as he appears in the Bournonville excerpt *Flower Festival* at Gensano

Scenes from *Walpurgis Night*. Bolshoi Ballet production: ballet music from Gounod's *Faust* provides the inspiration for a bravura display of pyrotechnics

Two spectacle ballets: *Petrushka*, created by Michel Fokine at the beginning of the century (above): *Spartacus*, a more recent Bolshoi production (below)

# *Modern ballet*

Martha Graham, the American high priestess of
modern dance (opposite)

Modern ballet – that is to say ballets created today in a contemporary style – borrows in large part from the classical and from primitive sources.

In America a large modern movement has grown up. Isadora Duncan was the first modern, she was a tempestuous and inspired dancer who also had a great influence on classical ballet.

After Fokine, the great Russian master, had seen her dance, he was driven to bring a new fluidity to the rigidness of the old classical style.

There followed after Isadora Duncan numerous American choreographers and dancers, and the greatest and most enduring of these is Martha Graham.

Martha Graham has created her own style, and she has inspired many disciples who are spreading the modern dance to many parts of the world. Merce Cunningham and Paul Taylor, two prominent exponents, have been seen in London and enjoyed success, although their success was more with the critics than with the general public.

Modern dance attempts many new forms; it uses atonal music and modern abstract painting. It uses distortions, contractions, and impulses. It has its own eccentricities and felicities of movement, but it is not readily acceptable to the lover of classical dance.

Nevertheless – the classical ballet is becoming influenced by new trends, the thirst for novelty at any price; the feverish search for the new and the original leads to many strange and sometimes incongruous innovations.

The trend is evidenced by the painting and architecture of our time. Obviously it is not to everybody's taste. The more conventional man will like the conventional ballet – the purely classical based upon the subtleties of the circle, whereas the young modernist, the *avant garde*, will take pleasure in the latest discoveries of the perverse symbolism of our age.

Whatever the trend, wherever dance and the art of ballet adventures, the basis of all dance and the backbone of a dancer's technique lies in the classical training. Tradition plays an all-important part, giving perspective, foundation, and momentum to the art – therefore in following the development of classical movement as set forth in this book, the reader will be preparing his mind for the receptivity of dance experience in its manifold forms.

Bearing in mind all the 'isms', the fetishes and fashions, the greatest joy in watching ballet, whether it be classical or modern, is to see beautiful movement, expressively performed, with technical skill and the soul of artistry. Audiences without any intimate knowledge of the technicalities will always be moved and uplifted by the spectacle of power and beauty.

Paul Taylor, American modern choreographer, shows that modern dancers can also get off the ground (above)

Merce Cunningham, modern dance choreographer from America, in his own ballet *Septet* with Carolyn Brown (right)

Alvin Ailey in American Modern Dance Works, a highly praised company. These pictures give some indication of the variety of angles which modern ballet takes in its stride

Striking pictures of Maurice Béjart's production of *Le Sacre du Printemps*. First produced by Diaghilev's company in Paris with Nijinsky's choreography, it created a furore. So loud was the storm of protest by the first night audience that the music could not be heard. Even today this erotic ballet is considered provocative and sensational

Opposite: Harlequin Ballet production of Lord Horder's adaptation of *Unicorn in the Garden*: Christine Barwick as the Wife, Donald McAlpine as the Husband, Jac Van de Veen as the Policeman. Even domestic comedy can be interpreted in balletic form with conventional mime

Walter Gore's *Street Games* performed by Western Theatre Ballet. An attractive ballet about children playing in the street

Harlequin Ballet presented a modern ballet in Coventry Cathedral (below). Yet another form in which ballet can be used

On following pages: *Pas de deux* by Alvin Ailey group, and the Moiseyev troupe from U.S.S.R. in *Football*. Even games can be represented in ballet form, as the Russians so vividly showed with their comedy piece

# ELEVATION

Much of the joy of classical dancing is in its lightness. The classical dancer endeavours to overcome the laws of gravity, to leap high and easily, to fly in the air.

The two pictures show how these male dancers have succeeded in cultivating phenomenal leaps, thrilling to watch.

Opposite: Dancer in class. Kirov School, Leningrad

Dancer on stage. Vilen Galstyan, Armenian dancer from Erevan, in Torch Dance

# *The Class*

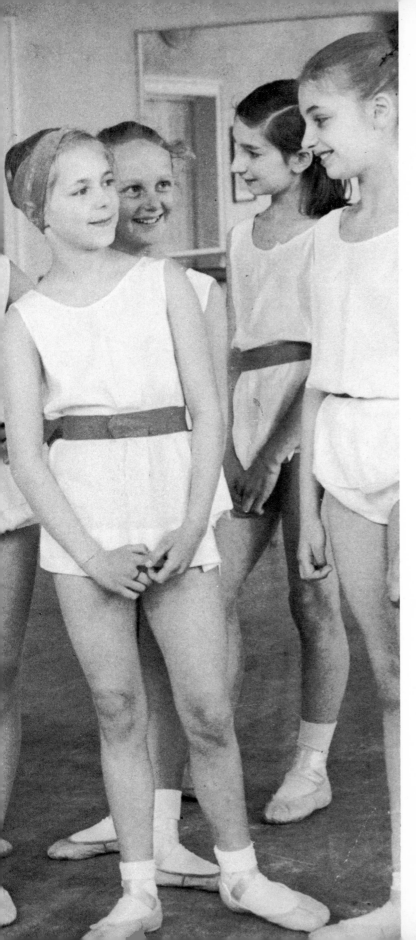

Royal Ballet children. A happy group of children at the Royal Ballet School, White Lodge, Richmond, where the raw material of ballet is moulded into the classical form

## THE BARRE

When we enter the ballet classroom, we see a studio, maybe a church hall or a cellar, with a *barre* running round the walls.

The *barre* is the dancer's prop. It has been called the scaffolding upon which the dancer's body is sculptured.

The first half-hour of the dancer's daily training is carried out, holding on to the *barre*, while she exercises one side of her body at a time.

Rudolf Nureyev, Russian, Erik Bruhn, Danish and Rosella Hightower, American at her famous studio in Cannes

## THE STANCE

At the beginning of her training the dancer has to learn to stand correctly. The placing of the hips, and shoulders, is the most important thing to understand. The hips must be directly over the feet; the back straight, the whole feeling in the body of growing-up, with the slightest inclination forward.

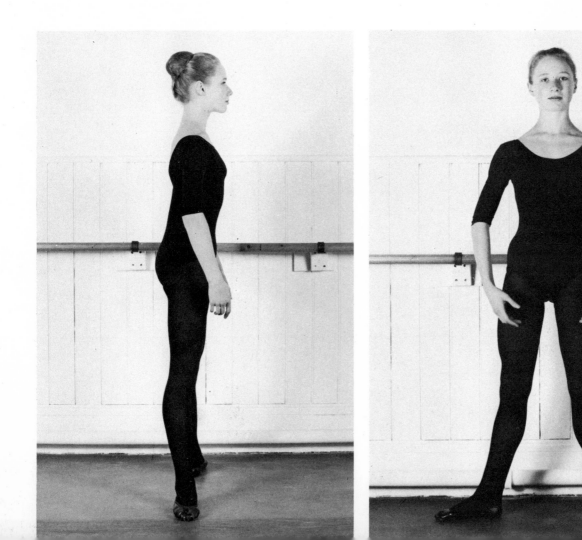

# TURN-OUT

The most important technical expedient of the classical dance is the turn-out of the legs from the hip to the tip of the toe. This unnatural opening from the groin gives beauty to the line of the body and is essential to the classical form. Apart from aesthetic considerations it gives the technical facility of balance and execution.

A lesson in turn-out at the Royal Danish Ballet School

# THE FIVE POSITIONS OF THE FEET

All the steps of the classical dance are built upon the five positions of the feet. From these positions the turn-out is forged. Only by the precise placing of the feet can the perfection and neatness of the dance be assured.

Jean-Georges Noverre, the great eighteenth-century ballet master, once wrote, 'The five positions of the feet should be thoroughly learned, and then gracefully forgotten about'. It is clear that there is far more to dancing than the five positions.

Top left: 1st position; top right: 2nd position; below left: 3rd position; below centre: 4th position; below right: 5th position

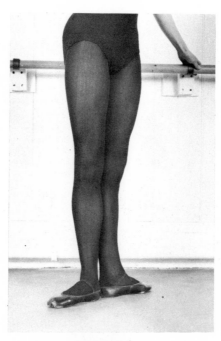
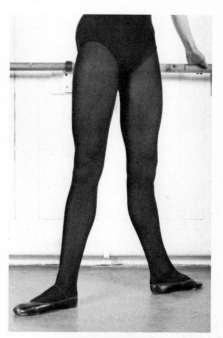

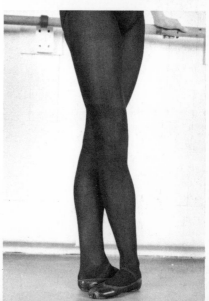

# THE FIVE POSITIONS OF THE ARMS

The dancer's arms give the final adornment to her movement. They must be trained to move smoothly, gracefully, and without reflex movements; always sustaining effortlessly the movements of the legs.

It will be seen that the five positions of the arms trace the pattern of a circle.

Opposite: a group of graceful arms in *Swan Lake*

Below: young pupils at the Kirov School

## THE CLASSICAL LINE

The plastic form of the classical dance is based upon the circle. If we examine any classical position we shall find that it is made up of parts of a circle. The positions illustrated show clearly the curves of a number of circles. It is these curves that give the harmonious grace and flow to the dance.

Where movement is square or angular, it shows the neo-classic or modern trend. It is not purely classical.

## EPAULEMENT

The *efface* and *croise* positions show the epaulement of the Russian school. The Russian masters discovered that by turning the body on the oblique greater elongation and refinement of line could be obtained.

Above: *arabesque effacé* on the *demi-pointe*
Below: *relevé effacé devant*

# THE PLIÉ

The *plié* is a slow bending and stretching of the legs in the turned-out positions. This relaxing and stretching of the legs should have a smooth, elastic action. It gives the first warming and preparation to the muscles and ligaments of the legs.

The illustrations show the dancer executing a full *plié* in the 2nd position

# DEMI-PLIÉ

This is a half-bend of the legs. It is the preparation of a jump; and the ending. It provides the impetus, and controls the landing. Without. *demi-plié* there could be no dance.

Illustration bottom right depicts *demi-plié* in 5th position

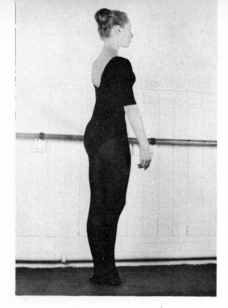  

## BATTEMENT TENDU

*Tendu* means stretch. The dancer's foot has to be an implement of strength and beauty. The *battement tendu* develops a beautiful curve to the instep, and a strong achilles tendon.

The illustrations show *battement tendu en croix simple*

## BATTEMENT TENDU JETÉ

A variation of the simple *tendu*. It is executed at a quicker tempo and gives dexterity and lightness to the dancers' legs.

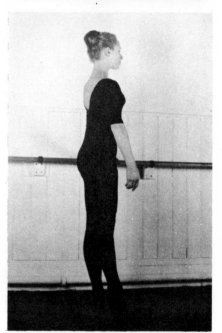

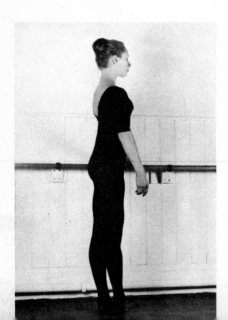  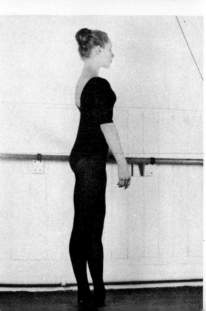

Right: a dancer's instep

Children at the Royal Danish Ballet School

# BATTEMENT FONDU

*Battement fondu* is a floating movement from relaxation to stretch. Bending and rising on one leg, as the other leg unfolds in an extended stretch to an open position.

This is one of the most important of all exercises because it cultivates a very rare quality—*'ballon'*—the soft alighting from a jump.

The illustrations show the dancer executing *battement fondu* in the *croise* and *efface* and *à la seconde* positions

## BATTEMENT FRAPPÉ

This is a strong sharp movement of the lower leg, which serves to strengthen the knee. It is also the basic action of *jeté*, one of the most frequently used jumping steps.

*Battement frappé en croix*

## ROND DE JAMBE PAR TERRE

Round of the leg. The tip of the toe describes a semi-circle on the floor. This exercise assists further the turn-out and control of the hips. It enables the thigh to rotate easily in the hip socket.

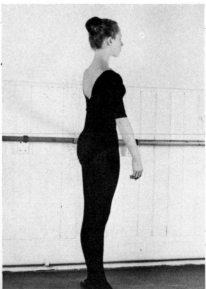

## ROND DE CUISSE

Round of the thigh. Often used in conjunction with the *rond de jambe*, it is a splendid exercise for rendering the hip joint supple, while strengthening the adjoining ligaments and tendons.

Students of the Bolshoi School, Moscow, being watched by some of their teachers

# PORT DE BRAS

Carriage of the arms. Circular movement of the arms which brings the whole body into play. This cultivates a fluid quality emanating from the centre of the body.

*Port de bras en dehors* and *en dedans*

## ROND DE JAMBE EN L'AIR

A movement much used in classical variations. Difficult and strenuous to execute correctly; it develops flexibility of the knee joint, and adjustment of the turned-out hip.

*Rond de jambe en l'air*

*Passé*

## BALANCE

After various exercises, the balance is held on the half-toe (*demi-pointe*) in *attitude, arabesque* or *closed* position (*cou de pied*).

The dancer illustrates some of the balancing positions.

*Attitude devant* (right)

*Attitude*

# DEVELOPPÉ

Called the *adage* of the *barre*-work because the movements are performed slowly. The *developpés* are the slow unfolding movements of the legs. The object is to lift the leg as high as possible, with ease and perfect control—to cultivate beautiful flowing lines. Noverre says: 'The consequences of false positions are fatal. Simplicity in any style demands the greatest perfection.'

Above: left, *passé*; centre, *developpé devant*; right, *passé*; below: left, *à la seconde*; centre, *developpé en arabesque*; right, *arabesque penchée*

Opposite: a pupil at the Bolshoi; 'The hard grind'

# GRAND BATTEMENT

A vigorous high kick with a stretched leg, that gives additional strength to the whole leg, and assists in giving more strength and suppleness to the groin.

*Grand battement devant* and (below) *Grand battement derrière*

Getting ready for class at the Kirov School, Leningrad

# PLIÉ-RELEVÉ

After the slow extensions and the high swings, a reworking of the instep and achilles tendon is carried out with a series of bend and stretch movements.

*Demi-plié* and (below) *Relevé à demi-pointe*

Barbara Vernon, teacher and choreographer

# STRETCHING EXERCISES

The exercises at the *barre* finish with stretching exercises, of which there are many. These exercises must be done carefully and slowly; they serve to beautify the body and keep the muscles and ligaments superbly fit.

The illustrations show various examples

Centre-practice takes place on the floor of the studio. The dancer having tuned her body at the *barre* is now warmed and ready to undertake an hour or more of concentrated work.

The regime in the centre will follow very closely the pattern of the *barre*-work, but will become more varied and strenuous. It will be seen that the dancer has to grapple with the obstinacies of nature, and battle methodically against the laws of gravity.

A description of the exquisite dancer Marie Taglioni, one of the greatest dancers of the last century, which appeared in the *Morning Post* in 1830, suggests a perfection for which so many struggle and few attain:

'She is a wonderful being, and realises all that the most sanguine imagination can picture of the poetry of movement. Her face is not beautiful, but her figure is a perfect model. . . . She has attuned that form to the most delicate harmony, and her neck, her arms, and feet are all inspired by the same elegance.'

Eager pupils at the Royal Danish Ballet School, Copenhagen

Two more examples of stretching exercises

Below: Svetlana Beriosova in a brilliant *Grand jeté*

# ADAGE

The slow movements in which the body is gradually transmuted and formed by a process of successive moulds into a refined and sensitive instrument.

Opposite: above, *attitude en croise*; centre, *écarté derrière*; below, *à la seconde*; right, *renversé*

Below: left, *arabesque en effacé*; centre, *arabesque en croise en perchée*; right, *arabesque allongé*

Senior girls at the Kirov School, wearing traditional pink tunics

# TEMP-LIÉ

(To tie) Passing the weight from one leg to the other, from bend to stretch. An important exercise that facilitates the easy flow of the movement.

*Temp-lié* to the side (right and middle row)

*Temp-lié en croisé en avant à la demi-pointe* (bottom row)

## ALLEGRO

This section of the class gives rein to a wide, expressive range; nuance, lightness, elevation, *ballon*–quick, lively, joyous movement; simple or adorned. Many of the steps may be embroidered with *batterie*–the beating of the legs together in the air. Note particularly in the *allegro* steps the play of the head and shoulders. It will be seen that the head is always slightly inclined towards the forward shoulder. In other words, although the body turns or half-turns, the carriage of the head is to the front. This contributes a stylish fluency that is particularly seen in Russian-trained dancers.

Above: Illustrations of *glissade* to the side
Below and right: *Pas de Bourreé* under

A fragment of Benesh Dance notation (see page 121)

BLUE BIRD, GIRL'S SOLO

From THE SLEEPING BEAUTY, ACT III.          Music - Tchaikovsky

Andantino

Students of the Royal Ballet School in action

# JUMPING STEPS

Top left, *soubresaut*, a spring from two feet in which the legs are held close in 5th position; top right, *chassé*, a gliding step in which one leg chases the other

Right, two soloists of the Royal Ballet executing a *cabriole*

# BATTERIE

The deft and brilliant beating of the legs during the quick movements of *allegro* can be magical to watch. The secret of superlative *batterie*, apart from the technical expedients of turn-out and stretch, is to lift the supporting leg to hit the working leg at the precise moment of elevation.

Above and right: *assemblé*, a jump in which the legs come together in the air

Below: *sissonne* (or *sisol*), a soft leap from two legs

Above: *coupé ballonné*, a sprung step that hugs the air

Left and below: *failli*, a flying step in which the back leg glides forward

Opposite, above and centre: *emboité*, a jumping step with a half-turn of the body. Frequently performed in series

Opposite, below: Royal Ballet students executing *échappé*

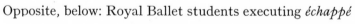

# GRAND SAUTÉ (The big jumps)

With the final phase of the class we come to the *tour de force*. The dancer attempts to defy the earth-bound fate of man; to fly like a bird, to sail on the air, to move like a goddess.

The gifted dancer with ample elevation is quite a rare thing. There is no greater thrill in the ballet than to see an artist propel herself or himself into the air with the feline grace of a panther. Only many years of training in a good school can achieve this phenomenon.

Opposite page: *Grand Jeté en arabesque effacé*. Left: *Grand Jeté en arabesque croisé*. Above: Bolshoi children at their lessons

# THE POINTE-WORK

Dancing on the *pointe* of the toe was an invention that first appeared in the early part of the last century and revolutionized ballet. Geneviève Gosselin of the Paris Opéra was the first known ballerina to appear on *pointe* in 1818. The fashion was quickly adopted by other famous ballerinas to enhance their grace, and give the illusion of weightlessness. In 1820 the great Taglioni appeared on *pointe*, and about the same time in Russia the immortal Istomina took to her *pointes*.

The innovation of the *pointe* shoe gave ballet a new distinguishing style, an ethereal glamour, a romanticism that could never have been attained by ordinary conventional means. But dancing on the *pointe* entailed more preparation and strengthening of the feet. Indeed many have suffered in the cause of beauty, and countless children have been deformed for life by being forced on to their *pointes* too early, and without correct training.

It cannot be denied that the *pointe* shoe is a cruel little slipper, with its hard back and stiffened toe-piece. All the same, with the passage of time and technical progress the shoe has become lighter and more civilized, and certainly teaching methods have improved.

Exercises in the centre for perfecting *pointe*-work: *échappé–relevé passé*; *pas de bourrée–assemblé*; *piqué en arabesque*; *piqué en attitude*; *rond de jambe en l'air* with *relevé*; *chaîne* turns; *piqué manège*; *fouettés pirouettes*. (For descriptions of the steps see Glossary.)

Exercises and steps *en pointes*: above, *échappé à la seconde*; below,
*bourrée*, a travelling step in which the dancer appears to float
*en pointe*

*Relevé passé*; from *plié* on two feet the dancer rises to the *pointe* on one foot

Opposite: *écarté*

Below: left, *relevé en arabesque en effacé*; centre, *relevé en attitude en croisé*; right, *relevé à la seconde*

# PIROUETTES

The pirouette is an acrobatic trick. It is used in the classical dance with great frequency and in a great variety of ways. Fundamentally the pirouette expresses excitement, exhilaration and humour. In its more elaborate forms it can have great plastic beauty. When used as a *tour de force* it can be breathtaking.

Illustrations show the *fouettés pirouettes*

# FOUETTÉS PIROUETTES

With the whipping of the leg the dancer
executes a series of turns on the point of the
toe.

Student dancers on the stage of the Kirov school, where Pavlova, Karsavina, Nijinsky
and latterly Ulanova and Nureyev danced their first steps

# Appendix

## HOW THEY PREPARE AND WHAT THEY WEAR

The dancer's equipment consists of practice clothes and shoes. Tights, leg-warmers and leotards are the most sensible form of dress for the classroom. Tights are nylon or wool; leg-warmers are of heavy, knitted wool, and are worn over the tights to generate and hold the heat essential to keep the muscles of the body warm. The practice tutu has been fashionable in many schools but it obscures too many faults to be a wise garment for training. In practising double-work (*pas de deux*) it should be worn so that the partner can accustom himself to the feel of the tutu.

### TUTU
The tutu is a creation of the Romantic Age. First popularized by the great dancer Taglioni, it has remained the accepted apparel of the classical dance. The Romantic tutu is long and soft, falling to mid-calf. It gives an ethereal effect. The classical tutu is short and springy. It consists of rows of frills of net fixed to a basque around the dancer's hips.

### SHOES
The soft ballet shoe or slipper is made usually of kid or leather; it should fit the foot closely like a glove, and has no heel.

### POINTE-SHOES (BLOCKS)
These are satin slippers the same shape as the soft shoe, but the toe-cap, from toe-tip to vamp is hardened with glue, and the sole of the shoe is strongly reinforced to give support to the arch of the foot when on *pointe*.

Mr. Selva the famous ballet shoemaker of New York says, 'If you practice every day you should alternate your toe shoes, and you will find they have a longer life.'

### MAKE-UP
Make-up for the stage performance is another important part of the dancer's presentation, and the ability to make up effectively has to be learned. Most often it is taught in schools, but a great deal can be learned by observing experienced dancers.

Make-up may be obtained from most large chemists or drug-stores. Some towns boast a theatrical shop, but failing this the ballet shoemakers in London and New York stock every requirement of the dancer and performer. See advertisements in leading dance journals.

## SCHOOLS, EXAMINATIONS, GRANTS

A great many schools of ballet exist throughout the country, and a number of large boarding schools where girls and boys may commence at the ideal age of eight or nine and have general education along with daily ballet training.

Many of the large schools make regular announcements in the dance magazines.

There exist a number of institutions for propagation and control of systems of classical dance. These bodies organize examinations, and sometimes offer scholarships for dancers who wish to learn to teach as well as dance. In Britain organisations such as The Royal Academy of Dancing and the Cecchetti Society, and in America Dance Masters and Dance Educators publicise events in the dance journals.

Most of the teachers of dancing belong to an examination body, and they are able to organize annual examinations for pupils who wish to participate.

Many Local Education Authorities are willing to assist a recommended student of dance, and a number of Major County Awards are made to dance students annually. It is believed that many councils favour grants to students who are bent on teaching, rather than studying for a stage career; the reason being that any career on the stage is precarious. In America a large number of grants for dance studies are made annually by the Ford Foundation.

Applications for grants are made direct to councils, and require the recommendation of the pupil's teacher.

# AUDITIONS

Auditions for entry into ballet companies are held at regular intervals. For entry to most companies the applicant has to first spend a period of training in the school either attached or associated with the Company.

Although the principles of classical dancing are the same in all good schools, the styles and preferences of each company vary considerably, and that is why it is important for the student to study in the school that serves the particular Company he or she is interested to join.

# BACK-STAGE

Ballet appears to be a glamorous art: but it is really a life of hard work, as these behind-the-scenes pictures would indicate.

The dancers' daily life is taken up with training, rehearsing, travelling, costume fitting, darning ballet shoes, dressing and undressing.

Right: costume fitting at the Kirov school

A dress rehearsal at Rosella Hightower's studio, Cannes

Paula Rufina darning *pointe* shoes

Opposite: Presentation of Awards by Dame Alicia Markova at the Annual Examinations, Arts Educational Schools

Making-up before the school performance at Kirov school

Opposite: above, Barbara Vernon and Donald McAlpine watching a rehearsal while some of the girls do their knitting; below, the Swans prepare

David Lichine and Miss Grace Cone auditioning children for his production of the *Nutcracker* for Festival Ballet

# Glossary of Ballet Terms

| | |
|---|---|
| *ADAGE* | Sustained slow movement evolving from one extended position to another. |
| *ADAGIO* | Supported work between boy and girl including lifts and pirouettes (*pas de deux*). |
| *ALLEGRO* | Quick light sequence of steps. |
| *ARABESQUE* | An elongated classical position when the dancer supports herself on one leg, the other leg extended behind the shoulder. Arms may be varied but usually reaching forward or upward. |
| *ASSEMBLÉ* | Basic step when the dancer pushes off two feet, at the same time brushing one foot into the air to assemble or join them again on landing. |
| *ATTITUDE* | Similar to *arabesque*: a position supported on one leg, the extended leg being bent at the knee. Arms again may be greatly varied. |
| *BALLET BLANC* | Traditional classical ballet, dressed in white. |
| *BALLONNÉ* | A jumping step on one leg when the working leg is thrown out at knee-height to return on landing with the pointed foot under the knee of the supporting leg. |
| *BALLOTTÉ* | A see-saw movement springing from one leg to the other with an unfolding movement of the leg outward passing up the shin through the knee to extension, and also in reverse. |
| *BATTEMENT* | A strong throwing movement. |
| *BATTERIE* | Beating—when the legs are caught together in the air. An embroidery or elaboration of a step when the legs may beat or change places in the air. |
| *BOURRÉE* | Running step performed by girls on *pointe* when one foot follows the other in quick succession and gives the appearance of gliding. |
| *BRISÉ (VOLÉ)* | A beaten step similar to *assemblé* but can also be done |

Tamara Karsavina rehearses her ballet *Harlequin's Serenade*. Age passes to youth the secrets of the art . . .

from one leg to one leg—when it is called *volé* (flight) and has a flying effect.

| | |
|---|---|
| *CABRIOLE* | A big beaten step when the legs are caught in the air, and then thrown to a further height before descending. |
| *CENTRE-WORK* | Class work carried out in the centre of the room as opposed to work done at the barre. |
| *CHAÎNÉS* | A series of turning steps in the 1st position mostly performed on *pointe*—which should run so smoothly as to look chain-like. |
| *CHANGE-MENTS* | A small jumping step in the 5th position, the feet changing place before landing. |
| *CHASSÉ* | A gliding step when the back foot 'chases' the front foot—the feet passing through 4th position *par terre* to 5th position *en l'air* continuously. |
| *CORPS DE BALLET* | The group or 'body' of the ballet. |
| *COU DE PIED* | The ankle or 'neck' of the foot. A position in which the pointed foot is often placed during the execution of various steps. |
| *COUPÉ* | Cut—when the weight of the body is transferred or cut from one leg to the other. |
| *CROISÉ* | Position when the working leg is crossed over the supporting leg, the body being turned *en diagonale* and the head looking over the forward shoulder. |
| *DE CÔTÉ* | A position to the side. |
| *DEMI* | A half position: *demi plié*—a small bend, *demi-pointe*—half point. |
| *DERRIÈRE* | Positions extended back or closed behind. |
| *DÉTOURNÉ* | A turn. |
| *DEVANT* | Position extended front or closed in front. |
| *DÉVELOPPÉ* | High extensions which are unfolded from the knee. The foot is brought from the 5th position to climb up the supporting leg (front or back) to the height of the knee, and then opens in any direction to a full extension. |

| | |
|---|---|
| *DOUBLE-WORK (PAS DE DEUX)* | See ADAGIO. |
| *ÉCARTÉ* | Extended position performed *en diagonale* when head, shoulders and legs are turned in the same direction. |
| *ÉCHAPPÉ* | Escapement of the feet. May be performed *sauté* or on *pointe* when the feet are released from a closed to an open position and return. |
| *EFFACÉ* | Position when the working leg is in the 'open' position, i.e. not crossed over the supporting leg as in *croisé*, the body again turned *en diagonale*, the head looking over the forward shoulder. |
| *ELEVATION* | Jumping steps (*sauté*). |
| *EMBOÎTÉ* | May be performed *sauté* or on *pointe*. The back leg passes to the front (under knee) in a continuous sucession of turns, a half-turn being made with each pass of the leg. |
| *ENCHAÎNE-MENT* | A series of steps put together to form a phrase or sentence of dance. |
| *EN DEDANS* | A movement inward, or turning inward towards the supporting leg. |
| *EN DEHORS* | A movement outward, or turning outward away from the supporting leg. |
| *ENTRECHAT* | A beat or series of beats or changes of leg whilst springing in the air. *Entrechat quatre*–two changes, *entrechat six*–three changes. |
| *ÉPAULEMENT* | Shoulder movement–the turn of the shoulder and head in relation to certain positions. |
| *FAILLI* | A flying step from one foot or two feet passing from *arabesque* through 1st to 4th position. |
| *FERMÉ* | Closed. Usually relates to a step finished in a 5th position. |
| *FONDU* | Melt. An exercise for the Achilles tendon to render it supple and pliable for jumps. The soft landing from a jump may be called either a *fondu* or a *plié*. |

| | |
|---|---|
| *FOUETTÉ* | Whip. Mostly associated with a series of whipping turns executed on one leg on one spot. By some considered a circus trick. |
| *FRAPPÉ* | A short sharp movement for exercise of the knee joint, executed on one leg, the working leg moving from the ankle to strong extension at knee height in any direction. |
| *GARGOUIL-LADE* | A combination of *rond de jambe en l'air* and *pas de chat*. |
| *GLISSADE* | A gliding step used as a preparatory push-off for a jumping step. |
| *GRAND* | Steps of big elevation or wide extension: *grand pirouette* –big turns, often executed by men in series either *à la seconde* or *en attitude, arabesque,* etc. |
| *JETÉ* | A jump from one leg to the other. May be made small, large or turning. |
| *MANÈGE* | A series of turns in circular pattern. |
| *PAR TERRE* | Steps performed on the ground. |
| *PAS DE BASQUE* | A basic step taken from the folk dances and refined for the classical dance by the turn-out and stretched toe. |
| *PAS DE BOURRÉE* | A step comprised of three small steps, the most commonly used being *pas de bourrée* under, i.e. step behind, to the side and close 5th position front. There are many variations, but in every case the first two steps are on *demi-pointe* and the third *en plié*. |
| *PAS DE CHAT* | 'Step of a cat'–in which both knees or legs are picked up thus imitating a cat's jump. They vary according to nationality, there being a distinct difference between the French, Italian, and Russian. |
| *PETIT BATTEMENT* | A little shuffling movement around the ankle, the movement coming from a loose knee-joint. A preparatory exercise for beaten steps. |
| *PIQUÉ* | A step from one leg *en plié* on to a completely stretched leg on *pointe* or *demi-pointe*. |

| | |
|---|---|
| *PIROUETTE* | A turn executed on one leg in any position. |
| *PLIÉ* | The bending of the knees–or the other half of any and every step–the balance of 'stretch'. |
| *PORT DE BRAS* | Carriage of the arms–which includes the body since the arms start from the centre of the back. |
| *RELEVÉ* | A movement from *plié* to stretch on the *pointe* or *demi-pointe* of one leg. |
| *REVERENCE* | The curtsy–or thanks of the dancer. |
| *RONDS DE JAMBES* | Circular movement of leg either *par terre* from the hip joint, or *en l'air* from the knee. |
| *ROYALE* | A beaten *changement*. |
| *SAUTÉ* | Elevation, jumps, etc. |
| *SISSONNE (SISOL)* | A spring from two legs to one or from one leg to one leg (a hop). There are many variations. Sisol is simply a Russian abbreviation. |
| *SOUBRESAUT* | A jump when both legs are held together in the air. |
| *SOUTENU* | A gathering movement from a *plié* to rise. May be straight *en face* or turned. |
| *TENDU* | Stretch. Basic foot exercise. |
| *TEMPS DE CUISSE* | A step emanating from the Court of Louis XIV. A sharp pick-up, a jab of the half toe in 5th position and a push springing away and closing in 5th. |
| *TEMPS LIÉ* | Basic step passing weight of body from one leg to the other by a smooth transition from *plié* to stretch. |
| *TOUR* | Step performed by men: a pirouette in the air. Executed with a jump from 5th position to 5th position, the feet changing places during the turn. |
| *TOURNANT (EN)* | Any step performed turning. |
| *VOLÉ* | Flight–applies to some steps which are much travelled. |

# DANCE NOTATION

One of the great problems of ballet has been to record its works. Many famous ballets of the past have been lost because they were forgotten, and those that exist today have been handed down by memory from one dancer to the next, and are frequently rearranged with every new production or revival.

Many systems of notation have been invented during the past three hundred years, but the most efficient and accurate method was invented as recently as 1947, by Rudolf Benesh, an Englishman of Czech descent.*

It has since been adopted by The Royal Ballet, and an Institute of Choreology has been set up to train notators or choreologers, who will study the dance through Notation and record the repertoires of the world's leading Ballet Companies.

**15**

THE DANCE OF THE CYGNETS

From LE LAC DES CYGNES, ACT II.                    Music - Tchaikovsky

Allegro moderato

---

* One other system called Labanotation is used extensively in Germany and America. Invented by the Modern Dance pioneer Rudolph Laban, the system is used more by Modern Dance exponents than by Classical Ballet.

Opposite: dancer studying Notation before the performance

# Books to Read on the Art of Ballet

## 1. HISTORICAL

Blaze-Castil. *La Danse et les Ballets depuis Bacchus jusqu'à Mademoiselle Taglioni*, Paris, 1832.

Louis de Cahusac. *La Danse Ancienne et Moderne*, Paris, 1754.

*Classici Choregrafii*, Moscow, 1937.

Mary Clarke. *Sadler's Wells Ballet*, Black.

Mary Clarke. *Dancers of Mercury*, Black.

Serge Grigoriev. *The Diaghilev Ballet, 1909–1929*, Constable.

Ivor Guest. *Ballet of the Second Empire*, Collins.

Ivor Guest. *Dancers' Heritage: History of Ballet*, Black.

Ivor Guest. *The Romantic Ballet in Paris*. Pitman.

Lincoln Kirstein. *Dance, a Short History*, Dance Horizons.

Lincoln Kirstein. *Three Pamphlets Collected*, Dance Horizons.

Prince Peter Lieven. *The Birth of Ballet-Russes*, Allen and Unwin.

Serge Lifar. *Ballet Traditional to Modern*, Trans. Beaumont.

Joan Lawson. *A History of Ballet and its Makers*, Pitman.

Agnes de Mille. *The Book of the Dance*, Hamlyn.

Iris Morley. *Soviet Ballet*, Collins.

Natalia Roslavleva. *Era of the Russian Ballet*, E. P. Dutton & Co.

## 2. BIOGRAPHICAL AND GENERAL REFERENCE

C. W. Beaumont. *Complete Book of Ballets*, Pitman.

Anatole Chujoy and P. W. Manchester. *The Dance Encyclopedia*, Simon & Schuster.

Victor Dandre. *Anna Pavlova*.

Michel Fokine. *Memoirs of a Ballet Master*, Constable.

Arnold Haskell. *Balletomania*, Gollancz.

Arnold Haskell. *Ballet Retrospect*, Batsford.

Odette Joyeux. *Child of the Ballet*, Trans. Haskell, Wingate.

Mathilde Kschessinska. *Dancing in Petersburg*, Trans. Haskell, Gollancz.

Nicholas Legat. *The Story of the Russian School*, London, 1932.

Paul Magriel. *Bibliography of Dancing*, New York, 1936.

Agnes de Mille. *Dance to the Piper*, Bantam Books.

Romola Nijinsky. *Nijinsky*, Gollancz.

G. B. L. Wilson. *Dictionary of Ballet*, Cassell.

## 3. PHOTOGRAPHIC BOOKS

*Baron at the Ballet*, Collins.

*Baron Encore*, Collins.

Mike Davis. *Ballet in Camera*, Oldbourne.

*Mike Davis at Festival Ballet*, Oldbourne.

*Mike Davis at Royal Ballet*, Oldbourne.

Mike Davis. *Princess Book of Ballet*, Annual, Fleetway.

Mike Davis. *Girl's World Book of Ballet*, Odhams.

Mike Davis. *Wonderful World of Ballet*, Odhams.

Arnold Haskell and Mary Clarke. *Ballet Annual*, from 1947 to 1963, Black.

Albert Kahn. *Days with Ulanova*, Collins.

Lido. *Serge Lido*, Paris.

Keith Money. *The Art of the Royal Ballet*. Harrap.

Michael Peto and Alexander Bland. *The Dancer's World*, Collins.

## 4. CRITICISM

V. Bogdanov Beresovsky. *Ulanova and the Development of the Soviet Ballet*, London, 1952.

Théophile Gautier. *The Romantic Ballet*, Trans. Beaumont.

André Levinson. *La Danse au Théâtre*, Paris, 1924.

André Levinson. *La Danse d'Aujourd'hui*, Paris, 1929.

André Levinson. *Les Visages de la Danse*, Paris, 1933.

Iris Morley. *Soviet Ballet*, Collins, 1945.

Iris Morley and P. W. Manchester. *The Rose and the Star*, London, 1949.

Valerian Svetloff. *Le Ballet Contemporain*, Paris, 1912.

## 5. TECHNICAL

Thoinet Arbeau. *Orchesography*, Trans. Beaumont, London, 1925.

Carlo Blasis. *Code of Terpsichore*, London, 1860.

Carlo Blasis. *Notes Historical and Practical*, London.

Erik Bruhn and Lillian More. *Bournonville and Ballet Technique*, Black.

Dolores Kirton Cayou. *Modern Jazz Dance*, National Book Press, California.

Tamara Karsavina. *Classical Ballet: The Flow of Movement*, Black.

## 5. TECHNICAL contd.

Tamara Karsavina. *Ballet Technique*, Black.

Leo and Janet Kersley. *Dictionary of Ballet Terms*, Black.

Nadine Legat. *Ballet Education*, Bles.

Jean-Georges Noverre. *Letters on Dancing and Ballets*, Trans. Beaumont.

Gertrude Shurr. *Modern Dancing*, Ronald Press.

Celia Sparger. *Anatomy and Ballet*, Black.

Olga Spessivtseva. *Technique for the Ballet Artiste*, Muller.

Agrippina Vaganova. *Basic Principles of Classical Ballet*, Black.

Jane Winearls. *Modern Dance*, Black.

## 6. NOTATION

Rudolf and Joan Benesh. *Introduction to Benesh Notation*.

Diderot et d'Alembert. *Chorégraphie ou l'Art d'Ecrire la Danse*, Paris, 1770.

Raoul Auger Feuillet et Dezais. *Chorégraphie ou l'Art d'Ecrire La Danse par Charactères, Figures et Signes Démonstratifs*, Paris: Chez le Sr. Dezais, 1713.

Ann Hutchinson. *Dance Techniques and Studies*, Dance Notation Bureau, New York, 1950.

Albrecht Knust. *Kinetography Laban* (unpublished).

Juana de Laban. *A History of Dance Notation*, Dance Index Vol. 5, New York, 1946.

## 7. BALLET JOURNALS

*The Dancing Times* – Monthly

*Dance and Dancers* – Monthly

*Ballet Today* – Bi-monthly

*Dance News* – American Publication, Monthly

*Dance* – American Publication, Monthly